Mode of Ministry:

Managing the Church To-Day

by
Ian Bunting
Southwell Diocesan Director of Ordinands

gb GROVE BOOKS LIMITED
Bramcote   Nottingham   NG9 3DS

CONTENTS

THE COVER PICTURE

is by Peter Ashton

First Impression June 1993

ISSN 0144-171X

ISBN 1 85174 239 5

1. INTRODUCTION

Early in 1993, the manufacturers of *Cluedo*, a board game that has graduated into a television game show, announced that they were eliminating the Reverend Green from the list of suspects. He was to be replaced by an aggressive business executive. In real life, clergy have rarely been suspected of murder. They have, however, been among the socially significant characters of British society, some of which are numbered among the characters of the popular board game. During the last hundred years, for instance, clergy have stood alongside other recognizable leader characters like military officers, professors and the leisured rich. They have been people to respect. This has changed with the contemporary challenge to established institutions such as the monarchy and the church. The manufacturers of the board game, for whatever reason, are beginning to reflect the change.

In this booklet, we look closely at the changing expectations which have accompanied the social character of the Christian minister in the twentieth century. The fact that today it may equally well be a woman is just one of them. Our perception of the church's ministry has always been informed by the Bible. Obviously, it has played, and continues to play, an important part in shaping our views. We shall see, however, that an over-simplified biblical approach obscures the way the biblical models have been interpreted differently within diverse historical and social contexts. Sometimes the interpretations have owed more to dominant leader characters of the period than to their scriptural forebears.

Christians are always trying to recapture the spirit of biblical leaders and to relate the church's ministry to them. The way we all try to emulate the example of Jesus Christ in this respect is one illustration. In fact, however, our biblical understandings of leadership have invariably been moulded by the social conventions of the times in which we have lived. The hierarchies of clergy in the medieval times, for instance, only reflected the secular power structures of the time. One of the purposes of the booklet is to look at the changes that have taken place in the social role of the clergy, particularly in the last hundred years, and to see what those changes tell us about the changing purpose and style of the church's ministries.

In the twentieth century, the models have followed each other with increasing rapidity. This, as much as anything, has both reflected and affected the self-understanding of the clergy and people. When the position of the churches in society at large was more secure, for example at the beginning of the century, the traditional role of the Christian minister was not threatened. For the last forty or so years, however, the clergy have been searching for a new integrity and credibility. Sometimes they have been influenced by other professions which find increasing acceptance and respect from the public.

In the latter part of this century, some have identified the therapist and the manager as two of the socially dominant leader characters who, in part, determine the direction of society. For instance, many see the doctor taking the role the priest used to have in the local community. The prominence of therapist and manager in leadership roles has influenced the clergy in their self-understanding and posed something of a dilemma. Is ministry to be associated more with the bedroom or the boardroom? Clergy can feel pulled this way and that.

These two characters have also had an important influence on the church's expectations of its future ministers. They have determined many of the changes which have taken place in the traditional curriculum of theological training. Hitherto, of the two, the therapeutic model has been the more acceptable, certainly to Anglicans. Much ministry both to individuals and groups has proceeded with a therapeutic goal in view. At the end of the century, however, theological trainers echo the concern of the wider church to give mission a higher profile. In this booklet, we reconsider the overlooked managerial model of ministry which is generally unpopular in the training colleges and courses.

The Community's Pathfinder

A theology of mission calls for an appropriate form of church to reflect it, and ministry to sustain it. Many welcome the quest for communities which will display the new life of the people of God. Such communities, base communities for instance, have compelling authority in the churches of the Southern hemisphere, and have much to teach the churches to the North. We shall refer to them again when we come to the specifically Christian characteristics of leadership in the church. The appropriate form of ministry to promote mission through building communities is a pathfinding ministry. To many, the community pathfinder will sound much like a good modern secular manager. We might ask, had he lived today, would Paul have carried a mobile phone and a fax machine? In his apostolic ministry, I think so. But building Christian communities of character calls for other managerial skills too, which he did not lack.

Safeguards are needed. We are not wanting church leaders to replicate the older model of the manager as problem solver, or the one who simply implements theory in practice. Above all, we need imaginative pathfinders who will work with the churches to find the way ahead. There is more to it than updating an old managerial model of leadership. Jesus Christ is the Lord of the church. As the go-between, the Holy Spirit is the leader of the church in the Christian mission today. The goal is not the success of the church but the coming of the kingdom of God. If the managerial model is to stimulate a fresh approach to leadership in mission, it will have to retain and develop its distinctively Christian purpose, style and way of working. We shall return to this in the last section.

2. MODELS OF MINISTRY

From the beginning of the church Christians have used models to help them explain mysteries, for instance what they mean by the nature of the church and its ministry. There are almost a hundred models of the church in the New Testament. There are almost as many models of ministry. Naturally, they reflect the models of the church. So, for example, the church is the temple of God and the apostle is the builder. Models, of course, have their limitations. They are representations of what Christians believe and not exact descriptions. It is therefore not surprising if it takes many models to convey the fullest possible picture of what Christians believe about such an important institution as the church and its ministry. In this short paragraph, for instance, I have already used at least six models. All but one, institution, originate in the New Testament.

Three problems with Biblical Models
Biblical models present us with a problem when it comes to understanding the nature of ministerial leadership. First, in every period of church history, they have had to interact with the dominant leader characters of the time. For example, for much of English history the parson was as much an appendage of the landed gentry as he was a priest in the church of God. It makes us reticent about adopting biblical models too glibly. They do provide us, however, with a useful tool for re-examining and checking contemporary models of ministry. These owe much to today's leader characters and we will look at some of them below.

Social characters have a history, just as models of the church and ministry have a history. Although biblical models have always featured prominently in the thinking of Christians, they have commanded attention with varying degrees of importance. A process of development and adaptation has taken place within the shifting social focus down the years. Social pressure as much as patterns handed down from the scriptures and tradition have determined the changes in the self-understanding of ministers. What we find is that there has been a complex interplay of biblical precedent, church tradition and social context. All three factors bear upon what is happening now. The first thing to recognize is that we have all been deeply influenced by the expectations surrounding the dominant leader characters of our times.

This is not to deny that throughout history, and continuing today, there are frequent movements which try to recapture the life and vitality of the early church's ministry expressed in many of the New Testament models. These models continue to be authoritative and formative for Christians. Many believe a return to them is the first priority of the church today. Many others believe they need constantly to be reviewed.

Secondly, although biblical models are precious to Christians, and have a timeless quality to them, it is not easy for us to use them without reading into them what we think they mean. For example, all Christians will value the model of the church as the body of Christ particularly in a day when we are seeking both a new sense of 'community', and new 'communities' to display it. We all endorse the body model, and the enabling role of ministry which naturally accompanies it. Nevertheless, two Christians from different traditions will have differing views even when they use the same 'body' model to describe the church. In short, biblical models, divorced from an appreciation of the church context in which they are used and understood, have proved too multi-faceted to be satisfactory as a way of distinguishing precisely what we mean by the nature and purpose of the church and its ministry today.

Thirdly, there is a recurring discordance between our theoretical and operative models. We all think one thing and do another. We have to test our theoretical models of ministry against our practice of ministry. For example, if, when ministers review the use of their time and the location of their work, they find it to be spent mostly in studies and in offices, with secretaries and a list of diary engagements, it says ministers are consultants and administrators. At the same time, should they be claiming to lead their churches in evangelizing and serving the world, then such a ministry is not being modelled in the congregation and there is a glaring discrepancy. Models are only useful if they touch contemporary reality and have some practical credibility.

> John has recently been appointed to his first incumbency. It is a busy parish. He spends most of his mornings dealing with correspondence, preparing for meetings, writing addresses, and attending gatherings of fellow clergy. In the afternoons he visits church members who are sick, and parishioners in their homes. In the evenings, he attends church business meetings and various groups for fellowship or lay training.

In college, John was introduced to many stimulating models of ministry outlined below. No matter to which model John feels drawn, he faces pressure to conform to the older models we associate with the parish priest. If John is to match his ministry to his new convictions, he is going to need the courage to face conflict. The institutional straitjacket is a tough constraint.

Evolving Patterns of Ministry

That the church quickly became a social institution is self-evident from a very early date. The seeds of it are in the Gospels, in the band of disciples with their embryonic form of organization. It is no wonder that Christians have added the model of the church as institution to the biblical prototypes. In the course of history, moreover, it has achieved more prominence than others. For the most part, the minister has been the leader of the institution. For example, until the Reformation, it was the priest and he was closely identified with the ruling powers. At the Reformation the presbyter took over. But the new presbyter was at first not very different from the old priest. In John Calvin's Geneva, for instance, the expectation that the preaching presbyter would rule was not much different from the community role of the old sacrificing priest. Of course, a real change had taken place but it took some time and the break-up of the protestant churches for models of ministry to emerge which reflected a changed relationship with the ruling powers. The priestly agent of the church militant on earth first became the minister of the universal word of God. Later, his ministry became a more sharply focused pastorate to the congregation of the faithful. He still held, however, a residual sense of responsibility for the whole community. Later still, the minister became the manager of an eclectic, gathered, congregation. Today, he or she is often the shepherd of a minority 'lifestyle enclave' within a largely alien environment.[1] In each period of the church's history, therefore, models of ministry have been evolving which have been intimately associated with the church's self-understanding within the social context in which it has found itself.

Professional Clergy

Nowhere has this been more true than in the Church of England. Change has been slow because of the attempt to retain some form of uniformity, the traditional link with the establishment, and the desire to preserve the social status of Anglican clergy. Since the war, however, the rate of change has accelerated. Anthony Russell, in *The Clerical Profession*, has traced the way the English parson, who in the eighteenth century had been an appendage to the landed gentry, became, in the nineteenth century in the wake of the industrial revolution, an achieving professional gentleman. He describes the clerical role of that period;

'It was the professional man, gentlemanly but highly skilled, cultured but technically capable, conscious of the service ethic yet making a good livelihood . . .'[2]

In the twentieth century, as we shall see, our understanding of the professions has altered radically. We are not now talking about a gentlemen's fraternity but a meritocracy. The professions have become the sphere of those who are highly skilled, trained and qualified to practise their art. Not surprisingly this has deeply affected the ministry of the churches.

In our time the social expectations of society about their leaders has caused considerable confusion and this appears in the popular literature and entertainment of the day. For instance, in Joanna Trollope's novel, *The Rector's Wife*, to the consternation of the parishioners, the clergyman's wife takes a job in the supermarket. It is socially unacceptable for the Rector's wife to be stacking shelves. If she has to find paid employment at all, it should preferably be invisible to the public.[3] The book nicely illustrates some of the turmoil of both ministers and people about the changing clergy role today. Nevertheless, in their self-awareness, clergy and others have been becoming much more flexible, perhaps just confused, in their appreciation of the role they are expected to play. The same is true of the function they are to perform. At any rate, we conclude the clergyperson, with spouse attached, is no longer one of the dominant social characters in English society today as in the past.

[1] Robin Gill, *Moral Communities* (University of Exeter Press 1992), p.52f. Gill compares definitions of a 'lifestyle enclave' with a 'community' given in R. Bellah et al., *Habits of the Heart*, (Hutchinson 1985) pp.333ff.
[2] Anthony Russell, *The Clerical Profession* (SPCK, London 1980), p.22.
[3] Joanna Trollope, *The Rector's Wife* (Bloomsbury Publishing, London 1991).

Dominant Social Character

Alasdair MacIntyre, in *After Virtue*, draws on the style of Japanese Noh plays and English medieval morality plays to make the point that in the social drama of any age there are dominant social characters with whom the audience, people in general, may immediately identify. We recognize these characters as socially significant and crucial. Role and personality are fused together to the extent that much hangs upon the sort of people they are, what they actually do, and how they do it. This is not so with respect to all occupations. For example, today, a dentist or a retired middle-class person could not be described as social characters in the same way as a top business executive or a leisured rich person. MacIntyre argues that certain specific stock characters tend to determine a culture. Illustrating his point historically, he instances the culture of Victorian England which was partially defined by the characters of the Public School Headmaster, the Explorer and the Engineer.[1] Russell's nineteenth century professional clergyman seems to fit in well with MacIntyre's perception of dominant social characters in Victorian England.

When Avery Dulles surveyed the dominant historical models of the church he offered a helpful Christian approach to the use of models. He argued that such models, always adapting and complementing each other, help to deliver us from the temptation to encompass the infinite character of the church within our finite structures of language. At the same time, 'models serve to synthesize what we already know or at least are inclined to believe.'[2] The same might be said of models of ministry.

Two American writers, Joseph C. Hough and John B. Cobb, on the basis of an unpublished work by Ronald Osborn, and prompted by Alasdair MacIntyre's reference to dominant social characters, identified an historical list of ministerial models.[3] They did it in the conviction that, in periods of American history, certain dominant and generally recognized types of ministerial character have emerged. They relate both to the Christian tradition and to significant social characters within society at large.

Leader Characters in the Church

Until the Reformation the institutional Roman Church ensured the prominence of the minister as *priest*. Hough and Cobb's list starts, following the Reformation and continuing until the nineteenth century, with the minister as *master*. The minister is the knowledgeable teacher of the faith whose authority derives from an authoritative body of literature and his mastery of it. This dominant character of the seventeenth and eighteenth centuries provides a model which persists to this day. With the changing situation of the churches, however, other ministerial needs have called its claim for priority into question. This has led, amongst other things, to a tussle about priorities in theological education. Bishops and other leaders used to think that the university was the best place to train future ministers of the church. Many still do. More do not. In 1993 for instance, the bishops of the Church of England 'agreed that a formal shift of responsibility for ordination training to the Universities is neither practical nor

[1] Alasdair MacIntyre, *After Virtue* (Duckworth, London 1981), p.26.
[2] Avery Dulles, *Models of the Church* (Gill and Macmillan, Dublin 1976), p.22.
[3] Joseph C. Hough and John C. Cobb, *Christian Identity and Theological Education* (Scholars Press, Chico, California 1985), pp.5-18.

desirable.'[1] In short, church leaders now look for a more practical orientation to the training of the church's future ministers. In the next section,
when we look at changes in Anglican priorities for ordained ministry, we
shall uncover the evidence for this claim.

In the nineteenth century, as Anthony Russell pointed out with reference
to the English clergyman, more functional types of leadership came to the
fore within a climate of religious pluralism. Towards the end of the century, the *revivalist* and the *pulpiteer* held the stage, in England as in the
United States. However, not all ministers had the particular gift of preaching. Yet it was a time of church expansion and great activity at the turn of
the century. The *builder*, the organizer and motivator of organizations,
emerged as a dominant social character. The model found its counterpart
in the life of the churches. Today, we would describe such ministers as
church growers. More importantly, a way, hitherto denied, was opened up
for women to exercise prominent leadership in the churches. Ministers
were expected to further the mission of the church by increasing con-
gregational numbers. They also had the opportunity, however, to
establish and maintain a whole variety of new church and para-church
organizations. These called for an increasing number of co-leaders, many
of the most distinguished of whom were women.

Meanwhile, the understanding of the *professional* was undergoing
development on the basis of a scientific interpretation of the universe as a
mechanical system operating according to fixed laws. Engineering and
medicine were the prototypical professions of the period. The pro-
fessionals, working from a corpus of scientific knowledge, applied
research-based theory to a set of problems. In time, they built up a
technology which could be taught to future practitioners. Not surprisingly, this had an increasing impact upon the self-understanding of
ministers during the early part of the twentieth century, and an even
greater one after the war. This influence, as we have seen, has met a con-
sistently strong rearguard action from theological trainers still committed
to the model of the institutional priest or the educated master. The resis-
tance continues today. John, the imaginary priest I depicted in his first
incumbency, feels the tension in himself and in his diary engagements.

By the middle of the twentieth century, trainers were generally recogniz-
ing the importance of professional competence. They were struggling to
balance the need, as they saw it, to lay a sound theoretical base for ministry with the increasing demand by the students and churches for more
practical training. In the event, as Richard Niebuhr was to point out, the
model of the minister as *pastoral director* gained prominence. The minister was pastoral, because he exercised a ministry of counselling the congregation, and, director, because he managed the congregation, often
from a desk in an office.[2] More recently, Alasdair MacIntyre has also identified two dominant leadership characters of the late twentieth century;

---

[1] The Archbishop of York's letter to Principals of Theological Colleges and Courses, 14
January 1993, Appendix 1, 'Educational Issues and Criteria for Assessing Theological
Colleges', (v).

[2] H. Richard Niebuhr, *The Purpose of the Church and its Ministry*, (Harper and Row, New
York 1956), pp.79ff.

9

the manager and the therapist. The *manager*, as he sees it, offers effective assistance to an organisation to solve its internal problems and achieve its goals. The *therapist* does for the individual what the manager does for the organization.[1]

Hough and Cobb identify a further contemporary model of ministry to which they attach great importance, the *practical theologian*.[2] The practical theologian, as they see it, is closely related to the modern manager in his or her pathfinding role. The manager is not the expert who has the solutions to specific problems. The practical theologian is not one who applies successful techniques to problems in the church. Practical theologians think issues through in the midst of Christian practice. They do it by themselves. They do it with others within the Christian community. They do theology in practice. Practical theologians therefore need vision and the ability to envision others. They exercise leadership from the front as well as in collaboration with others. They offer practical personal commitment to the mission of the church as well as the skills to enable others also to participate.

In these ways, the model of the minister as practical theologian reflects the modern managerial executive. Such a figure is certainly a highly identifiable and financially valued social and leading character of the late twentieth century. This character differs from Russell's nineteenth century professional because she or he is not a gentleman. Nor is it exactly MacIntyre's concept of the manager because she is a pathfinder as well as a problem solver and implementer of others peoples' strategies. This could be what Josephine Bax meant when she described the minister in terms of the keeper of the vision.[3] Practical theologians, like modern managing executives, have vision and insight. In addition to the other traditional managerial skills, they bring imagination and guidance to the practice of the churches. The model of the manager, as we shall see, has been singularly unpopular with the Anglican clergy. It seems that the laity think otherwise. In the Diocese of Southwell, for instance, wide ranging recent consultations about developing patterns of ministry have led to calls for clergy training in management skills. For good reasons, as we shall see, the churches are beginning to adopt the managerial model of leadership. The current implementation of appraisal schemes in dioceses is one piece of evidence. The question remains how clergy and people will perceive the role in the churches today.

One unmistakable feature of the last hundred years has been the rapidity with which new models have succeeded each other, and the confusion which has often followed as a consequence. We noted how this has frequently been reflected in the media presentation of the clergy person. We have been reluctant to jettison the old and accept the new. It is, therefore, one of the inevitable features of ministerial life today that Anglican clergy, like John, struggle to come to terms with the changing expectations of the

---

[1] MacIntyre, *op. cit.* p.29.
[2] Hough and Cobb, *op. cit.*, pp.90-94.
[3] Josephine Bax, *The Good Wine*, (Church House Publishing, London, 1986), pp.115ff.

church and society about them. It is hardly surprising that some ministers fall into a crisis of faith as they grow older. They find the churches looking over their shoulders at secular models of leadership which are generally welcomed by the young and the laity, and resisted by the old and the clergy. They discover that the expectations which they brought with them at their ordination thirty, twenty and even ten years ago have to be reviewed. For some, it was a call to be a priest or a preacher. For others, they saw themselves as a counsellor or an enabler. Today, are they to become practical theologians or managers of the church? Not only have their circumstances changed, the rapid turn-over in the models has increased the uncertainty of role and task. It is to those changing perceptions and priorities in the Church of England in particular that we must now turn.

Changing Anglican Priorities 1962-1993

There is a history to the models of ministry with which Church of England ministers have identified themselves over the last thirty years. It has been recorded in surveys conducted among ordinands and their trainers, as well as in other church reports. The ongoing tension between the Biblical models, those inherited from the past, the pressures of current leader characters, and the pressure of administrative responsibilities have led to a change in priorities. We shall trace the trends over the last thirty years.

1. In 1962 Towler and Coxon conducted a survey of ordinands' perceptions of the relative priority of ministerial roles. Because of the stronger position of the churches at that time, one might have expected signs of a more sympathetic appreciation of the organizational role of the clergy. In the event, the respondents placed the roles in the following order of priority;

Pastor and father of his parishioners
Celebrant or officiant at sacraments and services
Preacher of the Word
Counsellor, adviser and confessor
Leader of the local community
Administrator of church affairs
Official of the established church.[1]

We may note the low priority given to managerial tasks. It was late in the 1960s and 1970s that training for a more functional ministry began to make its mark in the timetabling of colleges and courses. This was the period when courses in counselling, group dynamics and management began to appear in the burgeoning curriculum of pastoral studies. But the therapeutic model took precedence.

2. Writing in 1964 and conscious of the declining influence of the Church of England, Leslie Paul noted the move within the English nation towards a more egalitarian society and the loss, in consequence, of the traditional professional standing of the clergy. At the same time he noted that prophetic voices were beginning to protest at the clericalization of the church,

---

[1] Robert Towler and A. P. M. Coxon, *The Fate of the Anglican Clergy* (Macmillan, London 1979), p.109ff.

11

and he foretold the new role of the laity as 'the religious revolution of the twentieth century.[1] Paul's particular brief and concern, however, was the deployment and payment of Anglican clergy, still conceived largely in their traditional role, as servants of the institution. In this respect, his report went nowhere near far enough in preparing the churches for the future which lay ahead of them, and which he accurately foretold.

3. Ten years later, in 1973, Andrew Windross conducted a survey of Anglican ordinands in which they were asked to place the various functions of the clergyman's role in order. 51% of the ordinands identified with an 'enabler' model of ministry, 37% with a 'minister' model (defined in the survey largely in terms of preparing and preaching sermons), and 12% with the 'celebrant' model.[2] In completing his survey, Windross administered the questionnaire, compiled by Coxon in connection with his research ten years earlier, to one in three Anglican ordinands in training. Commenting on the result, Anthony Russell said, 'there is an obvious social orientation in the "enabler" model with its commitment to people in the counselling situation and on the other hand to people in their social and political situations. It differs from the other two models in that it is people-oriented whilst the other two are church-oriented.'[3] The ministerial task is seen by the majority, therefore, as the development of Christians as people for service rather than as teaching the faith or ministering to the faithful. It foreshadows the personal growth dimension of the community development model of the 1980s, but hardly the good modern pathfinding manager.

4. Ten years later still, when John Tiller was writing in 1983, expectations about the clergy role were certainly changing again. He believed it was important to end the 'general practitioner' role of the clergy, for which it was by then impossible to write an adequate job description, and move towards specialist ministries, diocesan and local, which would harness, develop and use the unique gifts of each minister. This view emanated from a healthy dose of realism on the one hand and a new awareness of the laity, and their contribution to the life and work of the church, on the other. Clergy need no longer be expected to perform all the ministerial functions anticipated by the congregation. Job descriptions for clergy, therefore, should be drawn up so that it would be clear which gifts were required in the minister to be appointed.[4] Gifts for ministry were to be recognised and affirmed in all God's people, and the threefold task of all priests wherever they exercised their ministry, as Tiller saw it, was to undertake a ministry of prayer, to enable the ministry of the laity in the world, and to act as representative persons on behalf of the church and focal points of ministry within the life of the church.[5]

[1] Leslie Paul, *The Deployment and Payment of the Clergy* (Church Information Office, London 1964), p.92.
[2] Anthony Russell, *Two Surveys of Ordinands in the Church of England*, A Comparative Analysis, Occasional Paper no. 4 (ACCM, London 1976), p.4ff.
[3] *ibid*, p.6.
[4] John Tiller, *A Strategy for the Church's Ministry*, (CIO Publishing, London 1983), p.101.
[5] *ibid*. p.103.

5. In 1988 I conducted a survey of theological trainers in the United Kingdom in which I asked the principals of theological training institutions to prioritize the seven models of ministry, the origins of which I have explained above, and which I now list below in order of their historical prominence in England since the sixteenth century;

Priest
Master
Preacher
Builder
Manager
Therapist
Practical Theologian

When one compares this list with the role components in the 1962 survey, the most striking difference and addition is the inclusion of the practical theologian. Otherwise, there are strong connections which adds interest to a comparison of the results, even though the questionnaire was addressed to different constituencies.

As one would expect, there were a number of features in the result of my survey which marked off the Anglican trainers from those of other traditions.[1] In fact, there were quite marked differences even among the Anglican respondents themselves according to churchmanship. It seems best for our present purpose, however, to treat the Anglicans as a whole. In any case, there were some broad agreements across the churchmanship divide. For instance, all the courses and high, middle and low church theological colleges all gave a high priority to the minister as practical theologian. At the end of the twentieth century, this model of ministry has clearly captured the imagination of theological trainers.

Trainers from thirty Anglican institutions replied to my survey and placed the models in the following order of priority;

1. Practical Theologian
2. Priest
2. Preacher
4. Master
5. Builder
5. Therapist
7. Manager

A notable discrepancy appears here between the role of practical theologian which comes first and the role of manager which comes last. Respondents wanted clergy to be reflective practitioners or practical thinkers of the sort Hough and Cobb described when they defined what they meant by the practical theologian. In this sense, the respondents were moving along the same grain of current management theory which sees the manager as 'pathfinder'. However, paradoxically, they felt uneasy and had serious reservations about the more practical aspects of the role they associated with the unpopular model of the manager. Older ideas of

[1] Ian D. Bunting, *The Places to Train*, A Survey of Theological Training in Britain (MARC Europe, Eltham 1990), p.29.

the professional manager, seen principally as problem solver and implementer, die a slow death. Perhaps it is not so surprising because, in my survey as well as in other reviews, observers have noted the strong rearguard action being fought by traditionalists and those who want to recover the biblical models. Those who value the traditional models of ordained ministry as priest, preacher and master still want to lay a theoretical base for ministry. For them, this takes priority over the practical functions of the minister as builder, therapist and manager.

Here, therefore, is the critical evidence of the discrepancy between the theoretical and operational models of ministry in the churches of today. We ask ordained people, at least in parochial ministry, and, like John, they tell us that a large proportion of their time is spent in the day to day management of the congregation and its affairs. Clergy are filling the old style management role; solving problems, implementing strategies, organising programmes and controlling the process. However, this is not what most of them feel they want, or ought, to be doing. Reluctantly, they tell us, they have been labouring under an administrative burden to which they cannot easily relate their ministerial self-understanding. They prefer to be priests, preachers and practical theologians. Of the tasks performed by the modern manager, clergy prefer the pathfinding to the practical out-working of the project on the ground. Where it is possible they employ administrators to do the latter. Theoretical goals, albeit with an emphasis on the practice of the Christian faith, still head their list of priorities. This, at a time when, perhaps under the pressure of increasing financial and practical constraints, the administrative and management tasks of the church are undiminished in their demand upon clergy time and attention.

The Marginalization of the Clergy

The story of the churches' changing models of ministry has uncovered the loss of a clear sense of direction, and a lack of confidence in our patterns of ministry. It is not easy to say which came first. When the position of the churches was more assured within society at large, it was possible without much reflection to adopt and adapt the dominant social leader models of the time. More or less self-consciously, the churches reflected the leadership patterns of the society within which they were set and interpreted the Biblical models in the light of them. Now, the debate is much more open. Some try, as they see it, to recover the purposefulness and confidence of their New Testament forebears. Others seek models within contemporary culture which resonate with current Christian priorities.

At the same time, the clergy have become more church focussed in their ministerial self-understanding. Society about them has become increasingly secular. With the loss of their secure institutional role within the wider community, ministers have found themselves working more and more within the churches alongside the people in their struggle to make sense of the Christian mission in the late twentieth century. It is this ministerial priority which is revealed in the popularity of the model of the minister as practical theologian.

Further, ministers have related uneasily to the dominant contemporary leader characters of therapist and manager. At least they have been suspicious of the way that most people understand them. For example, by and large, clergy do not counsel except in crisis. Counselling has become a specialism within a structure for which most clergy have neither the time nor the training. They are wary about taking on a ministry which they know involves clear systems and outside supervision if it is to be done properly. Likewise, as we noted, most clergy try to avoid avoid administrative responsibilities. If they cannot escape them, then they protest that this is not what they were called to do. In short, clergy prefer to refer troubled people to expert therapists of one sort or another, and to find secretarial and administrative assistance with their practical managerial tasks. One of the consequences of refusing to relate more positively to dominant social characters could be further marginalization of the clergy. They could get squeezed out even more.

Ministry for Mission through Community Life

Where then does this leave us? The reports and surveys, to which I have referred, indicate that the churches have not given up, but have increased their concern to forward the Christian mission in modern Britain. Evangelization is the churches' priority for the last decade of this century.

Models of mission have jockeyed for prominence at the same time as we debate the nature and purpose of the church and its ministry. Here too, there has been a history. The 'creation' and 'proclamation' models of the last century yielded precedence in the middle of the twentieth century to the somewhat polarized 'prophetic' and 'pentecostal' models of the 1960s. In the 1970s the focus shifted more to 'incarnation'. In the 1980s, we began to see the hitherto somewhat muted 'kingdom' and 'redemption' models of mission underpinning reports such as *Faith in the City* (1985). The story has been one of ebb and flow.

The churches and their ministers, in other words, have been searching for suitable ways and means to pursue the Christian mission understood in different lights. When it comes to tactics, latterly, many have fastened upon the importance of building authentic faith communities. In many parts of the world these have proved to have the authority of a lifestyle which carries conviction within society, and convinces the honest enquirer. Such communities are outposts of the kingdom of God. They display the presence and redemptive power of God in their internal life, and and share it for the benefit of others. In this way they are sacraments of their model of mission. Some ministers are therefore making it a priority to acquire and teach the skills we associate with effective community developers. The purpose is to foster strong local communities which will prove the evidence of God to those who observe them.

Such a vision for the churches' mission and ministry ties in closely with the kind of hope expressed in the end by Alasdair MacIntyre. He too looks for new moral communities inspired by a new, if different, S. Benedict.[1] It is therefore interesting that this view of the church's mission is not as emphatically reflected among Anglican trainers as it is among others in the survey I conducted in 1988. Doubtless, the surviving institutional awareness, if not enthusiasm, of many Anglicans could explain this. Anglicans are among those most vigorously pursuing a rearguard defence

[1] Alasdair MacIntyre, *op. cit.*, p.244f.

of the institutional church, as of more traditional models of ministry.[1] The church as a community is less important to them than it is to others. The Church of England could learn much from those churches, including many Roman Catholics, for whom the community life of the people of God is the chief agent for the mission of God in the world.

We have been following a story of rapidly changing models of ministry. They all have something to offer, especially those which are rooted in the Scriptures and in the tradition of the church. Nevertheless, none is sufficient in itself. Each has to be qualified, adapted or supplemented. Changing times demand evolving models. Unless the church is seen to be the church for today, then the church is not the church at all. The church is the living body of our Lord Jesus Christ and we may expect the life of that body to be as visible, audible and effective as the church of Jesus Christ in the earliest years of its existence. If we are not as impressive as the early church, and we are not, it does not absolve us from searching, as they did, for the best models to express our mission through the life of the church and its ministry.

There are those who drive us back to the earliest biblical models. Their strength is that they serve as a constant reminder of our rootedness in the church of the New Testament. Their limitation is that we receive them always in the flawed context of our churches. It is dangerous to be wedded too closely to the models of the Bible and their imagined impregnable interpretation. We may fossilise the churches in a shape and style which cannot respond to the moving of the Spirit. We all know congregations like that. They have clung to a spirit of the past, thought to be biblically authentic, which once brought life. They often preserve or revere the name and work of one of God's faithful servants. Sometimes, they are relics of some past revival or spiritual renewal. The mission hall, however, has become more like a mausoleum. The church which once throbbed with new life has become a monument. The Spirit, as the Holy Spirit always will, bursts the boundaries by which bygone Christians attempt to preserve their unique encounter with the living God.

In contrast, the voices of contemporary secular prophets are also heard in the churches. A few of these, certainly in Britain of the 1980s, projected the entrepreneurial manager as the figure who could lead the churches as well as the country out of recession. Once again, we all know ministers who match the model we have learned to expect of the successful business executive. They stir us from the lethargy of complacent religion. As a measure of ministry, however, apparent success is a denial of the true nature of the gospel. Ministry is not a technique to be employed but a demonstration of God in the power of the Spirit.

Thirdly, we may attempt an integrative approach. It combines deep respect for the biblical models we have inherited and an appreciation that God's Spirit is still active in the world today, and not just within the confines of the community of faith. This should appeal to Anglicans. Part of our identity lies in our approach to issues. We try to achieve a coherent understanding of what the Scriptures say, as interpreted in our tradition, by the use of human reason enlightened by the Holy Spirit.

[1] Ian D. Bunting, *op. cit.*, p.21.

3. SEVEN CONTEMPORARY MODELS OF MINISTRY

Contemporary Christians use different models to integrate the theoretical and practical aspects of ministry. The models are manifold. However, the seven outlined below cover most of the strands of current thinking about ministry. Although they have elements in common there are also differences. Some, for example, concentrate on the minister in person while others concentrate on the congregation and the community as the point of reference. All attempt to integrate the thinking and the practice of the ministry. In this, they reflect the advance that has been made from the days, not so distant, when theory and practice were separated. Sometimes theory and practice were held to be distinct from each other, for example when theological education took place in the university and ministerial training in the theological college or parish. Since those days, theory and practice have vied for the pre-eminence in the curriculum of the theological colleges and courses. The debate has been lively over the last thirty years, and still continues. In the final section of the booklet, we shall try out another model which, while having common links with the seven which follow, has some distinctive qualities.

1. *The Consultant*
Wesley Carr has proposed a consultancy model of ministry. The consultant is normally thought to have more competence, skill and knowledge than other practitioners. Carr sees the consultant less as an expert and more as an interpreter. The consultant holds 'a point of reference which transcends what is immediate without becoming detached from what is happening.[1] The priest is, therefore, the interpreter through whom the people may integrate their experiences of life and faith.

2. *The Overseer.*
Christopher Moody has proposed a model of pastoral leadership which he describes as 'oversight'. He rejects the common idea of an authority figure. He sees the overseer as one who has 'an overall view of what is going on; which means staying on the edge, not being at the centre.[2] The watcher or shepherd, by the oversight model, is one who has the necessary insight to facilitate change and growth.

3. *The Competent Professional.*
Paul Avis has re-affirmed a professional model of competent ministry—'that competence comprises both specialized knowledge and the skills to apply and communicate it.[3] He believes that competence is a form of authority which gains respect in the modern world. We live in a climate where it has been tempting to reduce the academic content of training in order to advance the more vocational elements. Avis sees it as important to retain a proper balance between academic and technical competence.

---

[1] Wesley Carr, *The Priestlike Task* (SPCK, London 1985), p.15.
[2] Christopher Moody, *Eccentric Ministry* (Darton, Longman and Todd, London 1992), p. 88.
[3] Paul Avis, *Authority, Leadership and Conflict in the Church*, (Mowbray, London 1992), p.106.

4. *The Practical Theologian*.

Hough and Cobb understand the ministerial task as that of the practical theologian. First, the minister is a 'practical Christian thinker' fulfilling a pathfinding role in ministerial leadership. Secondly, the minister is a 'reflective practitioner' who helps the institutional church 'to find and implement solutions to practical problems as efficiently as possible.[1] The model of practical theologian draws together the distinctive base and the reflective style which is appropriate to Christian leadership within the churches. Hough and Cobb emphasize the importance of vision, aggressive leadership and commitment on the one hand and collaborative and enabling style on the other. They are, however, very eager not to lose the distinctive character of the Christian practice of leadership by allowing professional activities of a ministerial sort to gain autonomy from practical Christian thinking.

5. *The Minister in Community (Koinonia)*.

Alastair Campbell calls for a new and different professionalism which he describes as a ministry of love. Without denying the need for professionalism in the sense of special knowledge, skills and dedication, he would like to see it focussed on the formation of the whole church in shared fellowship and service. Ordained ministers, in their own persons, should not be allowed a guarded status or a dominant role;

Instead, leadership in *koinonia* and *diakonia* should be sought from the whole membership. Rather than seeking a specialist counselling role, clergy should specialize in the pastoral aspects of their preaching and priestly functions and should use their position of leadership in the congregation to encourage the caring ministry of all Christians.[2]

6. *The Community Builder*

Robin Gill has not so much called for as suggested another, worship community building, model of ministry. He sees the church as called to worship and to care. The two are intimately connected. 'Care is an expression of how we believe things are at their most profound level.'[3] The goodness which is beyond self-interest, which he seeks, is embedded in worship, and worship is rooted in communities of faith. The growth of such communities calls for talented priests, preferably not in extra-parochial and cathedral appointments. Gill believes this is where they tend to be found at present. He wants to see them on the ground in the parishes.[4] Many will dispute the point he makes about the current location of talented clergy. They will, however, heartily endorse his desire to see their energies devoted, in part at least, to community building on the ground.

[1] Hough and Cobb, *op. cit., p.81.*
[2] Alastair Campbell, *Paid to Care: The Limits of Professionalism in Pastoral Care* (SPCK, London 1985, p.107).
[3] Robin Gill, *Moral Communities* (University of Exeter Press, Exeter 1992), p.80.
[4] Robin Gill, *The Myth of the Empty Church* (SPCK, London 1993), p.286f.

7. *The Middle Manager.*
John Finney believes it is hard to better the description of most Christian ministers as 'the man in the middle'. Like middle managers they have to be mediators of change.[1] Within the range of models, he sees this as summing up well the four key and interlocking biblical concepts; servant, shepherd, steward and overseer (*episcopos*). Middle managers are to keep the vision of the church before the people. They earth it by showing them the path ahead and enabling them to follow it.

A Critique
Before too eagerly embracing any model of ministry we must consider its limitations. None are wholly satisfactory. Some models of ministry owe too much to the clerical paradigm within which they are trapped. In other words, they focus too much on the clergyperson. They reflect the way theology in the church, for the last hundred years, has become too closely associated with the training and work of clergy. The danger of the competent professional model of ministry, for instance, is that it tends to promote the ministry as an elitist vocation. Specialized knowledge and skills are centred in one person who enjoys the security of an enclave or guild of fellow-professionals. The call for a new professionalism closely interconnected with the community in which ministers serve improves on the old idea. Ministers are less likely to become the institution's functionaries or technicians. The models of consultant and overseer carry with them a similar danger. Emphasizing the responsibility of the clergy to be independent and to think creatively, they nevertheless hint at a ministerial detachment. It may not be old-fashioned professionalism. Without qualification, however, the models suggest distance, even if the purpose of the distance is in order to enlarge the limited insight and experience of the people. By contrast, the new professionalism envisaged by Campbell clearly centres the whole concept of ministry not in the individual *per se* but in the church community as a whole. In this, he shares with Gill a strong conviction that the minister is, in a non-technical sense, a community developer. This is one of the skills, though by no means the only or the most important one, required in a good manager today. The model which matches best a theology of mission and expresses itself in the tactic of community building is the *minister within the community*.

Secondly, some models of ministry are too exclusively church-oriented. Where forms of ministry do not revolve too much around the skills or insight of the individual minister, they may revolve too much around the life of the church. The temptation subconsciously to embrace current inward-looking perceptions is strong in a pluralistic climate. Too easily people assume the church is either a 'life-style enclave' to be maintained and expanded or an established institution, like the Church of England, somewhat protected within the surrounding alien culture. Such assumptions surface in views of the minister as the middle manager and even as practical theologian if we think of the congregation as the setting for ministry. An Anglican report remarked on this danger in the responses of colleges and courses to questions put to them in 1987 about the nature of

[1] John Finney, *Understanding Leadership*, (Darton, Longman and Todd, London 1989), p.4.

ordained ministry;

> 'The ordained as "leaders" can easily come to be seen as a Church-focused ministry, lacking a sense of being directed outwardly to the community, the society and the world. Again the emphasis upon the ordained as 'enablers' of the laity could restrict the clergy to operating largely in relation only to churchgoers.[1]'

Gill is well aware of this danger and goes to some lengths to define the focus of ministry as ministry in open-ended communities rather than bounded lifestyle enclaves. The minister is largely responsible for the character of the church within which he or she is the *community builder*.

Thirdly, consciously or unconsciously, the churches have been so wedded to clerical and church-focused ministries, and appropriate ecclesiastical models for them, that they have been unwilling to own dominant leader characters of the twentieth century. These, one suspects, have been tainted. It might be more accurate to say that they have been afraid of them. For instance, clergy in general, and Anglicans in particular, have always been reluctant to embrace the managerial model of ministry. Only quite recently has the model been taken up and defended whether as middle manager or, better, practical theologian. The manager as one of the dominant leader characters of the period, however unpopular with the clergy, has made its impact in the laity's understanding of what it means to be a minister. The minister is a *good manager*.

There is another dominant social character of our time to which we have alluded; the therapist. This model has been more influential in the church than the manager, but hardly more popular with the clergy in general. Most clergy still prefer to think of themselves as priests and spiritual directors rather than counsellors. Nevertheless, pastoral studies in colleges for instance took on a therapeutic character in the 1960s which persists today. I remember when I was revising the pastoral studies programme in Durham in 1971 the then Dean of Durham assumed, wrongly as it happened, that it would major on pastoral counselling. It was, however, a period when therapies of various types, such as 'Clinical Theology', seemed to build a bridge between medicine and religion. If not too many clergy gave up their orders for it, it did seem to offer a path to a new credibility and acceptance in the wider community. More than that, secular non-directive approaches to counselling and group work fed through to individual ministerial self-understanding and practice. Some contemporary models, the consultant for instance, still betray the effect. The minister is a *healer*.

All the models surveyed try to integrate biblical prototypes, church tradition and current perceptions of leadership. Those who use them have a shared purpose to build communities of Christian character, even if they differ in emphasis and style. In working to this end, they invest the models with characteristically Christian components. In the final section, I look at what I believe to be the best contemporary model of ministry and the specifically Christian responsibilities which accompany it.

---

[1] *Ordination and the Church's Ministry* (ABM Ministry Paper No. 1, April 1991, Church House, Westminster), p.43.

4. PATHFINDER

The attempt to integrate biblical models of ministry with traditional interpretations and dominant contemporary leader characters is an important
enterprise for the churches. It is consistent with an Anglican approach to
mission. Unable to escape the influence of dominant social characters, the
clergy have found the model of therapist more congenial than the
manager. However the managerial model has undergone a transformation
which has perhaps been more radical than its therapeutic partner. The
good manager is now recognised as a pathfinder. This allows us to take
another look at the idea, in relation to the leadership required of the
church's ministers.

It is not clear, however, that the Church of England is ready to do so. In my
work as a Director of Ordinands, I have found that candidates who are
managers in their secular vocation have often received poor reports from
national selectors. Sometimes it has been said that they lack sensitivity
and pastoral skills. Although neither their home parishes nor I have always
agreed with the judgment, it seems they have come across as aggressive
and goal-oriented achievers in the managerial rather than the more acceptable therapeutic mode. Obviously, my assessment is impressionistic. I
have, however, heard a senior selection secretary say that most candidates at conference seem more gifted for maintaining the church's
existing life than for extending it in mission.

We will need to be careful in the use of the model of manager. The clergy
person rightly resists the role of the functionary or technician of the
church. Nor is the church, as Anglicans see it, a discrete and bounded
human institution. There are therefore some negative and positive
qualities which distinguish the Christian minister from his or her secular
colleague in management.

Theological Suspicion
A theological suspicion of secular practice is entirely appropriate. For
example, regular appraisal of the clergy is currently becoming general
diocesan practice. This has been adopted from the secular business world
and could easily become another reinforcement of the clerical paradigm,
especially when such appraisals are normally conducted by clerical
superiors. A job description and an appraisal on that basis is not, one suspects, the best way to facilitate the pathfinding manager in the
church.

Again, for example, we need to ask whether the proponents of an
evangelistic technique, church growth for instance, are not in danger of
adopting uncritically a successful formula which owes only little to
Christian theological insight. The larger questions of the Christian mission
and its theological foundations may not be addressed. More of that below.
I often remember the Christ-like sentiment of Bishop E. W. Barnes of Bir-
mingham who once said, 'When it comes to religion, nothing fails like
success'.

A danger with too ready an acceptance of dominant secular models is that we may overlook the implicit theology which underpins them. We may fail to bring a Christian critique to bear. For example, the churches in the last forty years have adopted and adapted a therapeutic model of pastoral ministry. I suspect they have allowed it unbalanced importance in the criteria for the selection of the church's ministry, and in the programmes of pastoral training. Such an approach has been consistent with a theology of immanence and incarnation. However, it has sometimes been at the cost of transcendence, the beyond in the midst, as well as a complementary theology of the cross and resurrection. One consequence is that the church has become very inward-looking and problem oriented. Analysis of the problem has been of the first importance. Healing and wholeness has been sought in the inner resources of the hurting individual or group. Pastoral theologians have tried to point to a divine resource, the wounded healer, the God alongside and within. Such an insight has helped to deliver the therapeutic model from thrall to its more secular expressions. Yet, a rounded theology should make us more open to the complementary theology underpinning the way of the good manager.

Imaginative Leadership

More important than preserving a healthy suspicion about the secular therapeutic model is the need to examine the theological character and underpinning of the managerial model. The concept of the minister as a practical theologian is the way we have tried to do it in this booklet. It distinguishes the clergy from their secular managerial colleagues, even where they share the same emphasis on pathfinding. But it is more than a question of integrating theology in practice. The character of the practical theologian and Christian pathfinder comes out in the exercise of three distinctive responsibilities.

First, *the pathfinder is committed to establishing the identity of the church by telling the Christian story and interpreting it for the community of faith*. For example, it is important to keep the memory of the history of God's people and their leaders alive. As preacher and master of the word of God, the minister puts the present life and practice of the church to the touchstone of our biblical forefathers and those who followed in their steps. 'Remember your leaders, who spoke God's message to you. Keep before you the outcome of their life and follow the example of their faith' (Hebrews 13.7). The pathfinding manager of the church today, therefore, has a story tell, an identity to preserve, and a goal to pursue, which is much bigger than the current concerns of a local congregation. It is hard to overemphasise the importance of Christians knowing where they have come from as the basis of knowing where they are going. Every church, local as well as global, needs a history. For instance, I have been much impressed by the base communities' insistence that at their meetings the Bible is studied, and the life-story of the community is recorded. Pathfinding Christian ministry demands a sense of history.

Secondly, *the pathfinder leads the people in worship*. Most helpfully, Gill has emphasized the importance of this. It follows naturally too from the thrust of the previous paragraph. In worship, the people plumb the depths of their identity and draw on the resource that gives them strength for their daily living. It is more than telling the story. It is praying and singing the story and praising God for its contemporary relevance and ongoing power to save. Once again, I have been most impressed by the insistence of the base communities that at their meetings they always sing Christian songs and hymns. As leader of worship, the minister is not at all an appendage of either the social or the religious hierarchy. The minister is a person who enables the community to worship God and draw on the resources of the Christian church. Moreover, the lifeblood of the Christian faith is for all. The purpose of the minister in leading worship is to help the life of God flow through the witness and fellowship of the church for the benefit of all.

Thirdly, *pathfinding leadership calls for the use of theological imagination.* Theological imagination is nurtured in at least three disciplines. Personal spiritual discipline anchors the minister in God. Christ-centred and Bible-based independence of mind leads to discernment. A firm grasp of the Christian vision and hope helps to clarify long term goals and more immediately achievable targets. The models which have been used to express the importance of transcendence or eccentricity in ministry contribute to this emphasis. Better still, the model of the pa hfinding practical theologian, as we have seen, aims to integrate practice and theology. A progressive spiral of vision, discernment and engagement then leads both the minister and the Christian community forward in mission. The pastoral agents of base communities use this process to find the mind of God and to move forward in solidarity with their people. It is a recognition of the activity of the Spirit in the leadership of the church today as in the church of the New Testament.

I have deliberately used the leadership of base communities in the third world to illustrate the Christian characteristics of the community's pathfinder. Obviously, the setting is different in the western world in general and the Church of England in particular. Nevertheless, whether we think of a small local Christian congregation in an urban priority area or a larger suburban parish church, a deanery or a diocese, we aim to build communities. Effective pathfinding leadership of the churches will be formed on the same principles, and marked by the same Christian character.